The 30 Day Writing Workout for Entrepreneurs

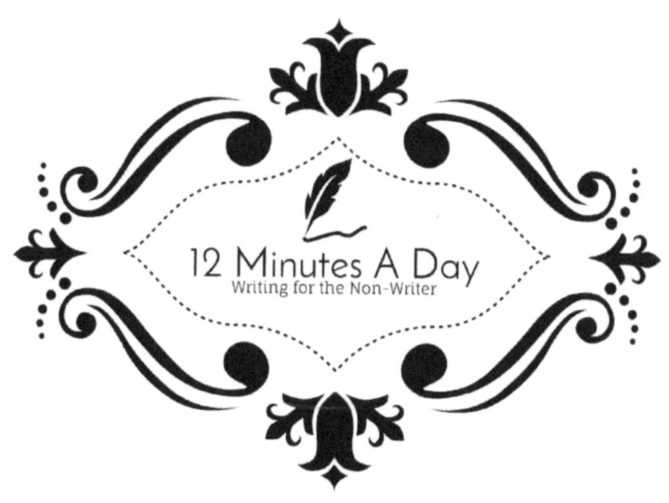

The Blogging Edition

By Renee Settle

ISBN- 978-1540701282
ISBN- 154070128X

DEDICATION

For those of us who are just starting and want to DIY with purpose.

Thank you for the lessons I learned while writing this workbook..

Your story matters. My story matters. Together, our stories will change the world.

12 MINUTES A DAY FOR ENTREPRENEURS INSTRUCTIONS

An introduction to the 12 Minutes A Day method for entrepreneurs!
I've used the 12 Minutes A Day method for many different exercises. Some 12MAD methods include questions to answer.

Tools you will need:

- A pencil, a pen, crayons, or colored pens or pencils. Whatever you feel most comfortable with using. You can even use a computer. The key is to make sure you are comfortable. I recommend hand writing it the first time because it will help you slow down and think. Sometimes our lives get so urgent that we don't take time to think. This process will help you take just twelve minutes to focus on one thing and complete it successfully.
- A way to time yourself. You will use something that will alert you at the end of two (2) minutes and ten (10) minutes. A smart phone usually works well for this. However, I've known people who use an egg timer shaped like a rooster. Whatever makes it fun and relaxing for you is important.
- Bring your imagination, because it will grow as you write.

That's IT! Just those three things.

NOW, here are the steps. Each day, you will practice these steps. So don't worry about getting it right the first time.

Practice Makes Perfect!

1. Open the book to the prompt you'll be working on.
2. Read the prompt carefully and make sure you understand it.
3. Set the timer for two (2) minutes.

4. Start the timer and draw a picture representation of what the prompt makes you think of. It doesn't have to be perfect or even understandable to anyone else. The key point here is to draw something you can relate to the topic. We are giving your brain time to process the prompt.
5. When the timer alerts, evaluate your drawing. Is it complete to your satisfaction? If it's not, reset the timer repeat step four (4). Do not stop drawing until the timer alerts you. Even if you trace over the same drawing, don't stop until it rings.
6. Now, review your drawing and reset your timer for ten (10) minutes.
7. Start the timer and write the blog that goes with the prompt. Whatever you do, don't stop writing. If you get distracted, write the thoughts in your head. Keep writing until the alarm rings.
8. If you haven't finished your thoughts, reset the timer and repeat step seven (7) until you feel comfortable. You may use other paper if there isn't enough room in the workbook. .

Remember, this takes practice, so if you aren't done after twelve (12) minutes, set the timer for another twelve (12)) minutes and keep writing.

CONGRATULATIONS!

YOU'VE WRITTEN FOR 12 MINUTES!

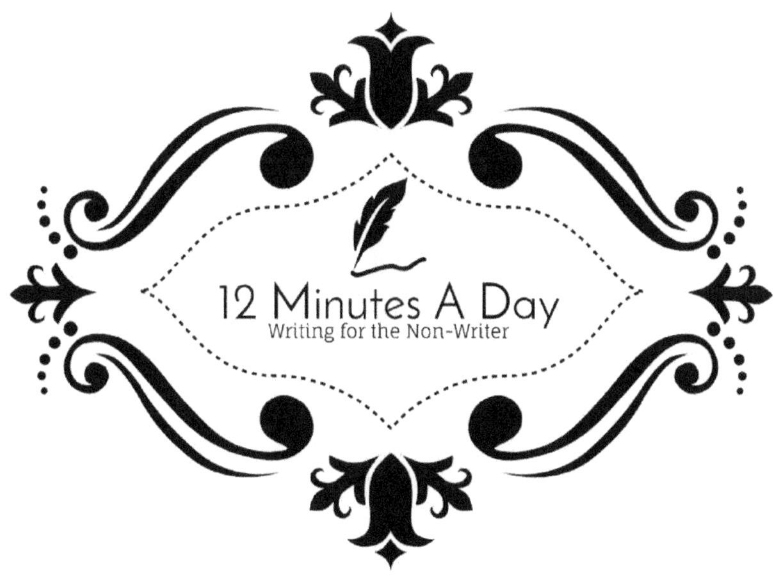

PLEASE NOTE:

1. This exercise isn't about good grammar, sentence structure or spelling. It's about writing down the idea, first. You can always go back later and edit it.
2. These steps are flexible. If you already know what you want to write and you think it's not necessary for you to draw anything, then set your timer for twelve (12) minutes and go to town! The idea is to write a blog. This tool set is designed to help you break free of a block. That means if you don't have a block and you just needed the prompt, then, this method has still worked!

JUST WRITE IT!

Once you're done with the workout, you can go back to each blog and edit, refine, add to, or take away from what you've written. You can even send it out to be edited. I'll be happy to help you with that. My contact information is on the last page.

Now you're ready to write your blogs!

NUMBER 1

Why did you decide to start your business? Write as if you're telling your best friend.

DRAW IT BELOW

WRITE THE BLOG

NUMBER 2 

What is your favorite tool, either online or offline, to use for your business?

DRAW IT BELOW

WRITE THE BLOG

NUMBER 3 

If there was one talent you wished you had, what would it be and why?

DRAW IT BELOW

WRITE THE BLOG

NUMBER 4 

What's your favorite holiday? Why? What do you like most about it? How does it make you feel?

DRAW IT BELOW

WRITE THE BLOG

NUMBER 5

Write your vision statement, then write an example of how it's used in your business.

DRAW IT BELOW

WRITE THE BLOG

NUMBER 6

What is your favorite business quote? Write the quote and why it applies to your life.

DRAW IT BELOW

WRITE THE BLOG

NUMBER 7 

Define an overall problem you've seen over time in your business. Then write your idea to answer that problem.

DRAW IT BELOW

WRITE THE BLOG

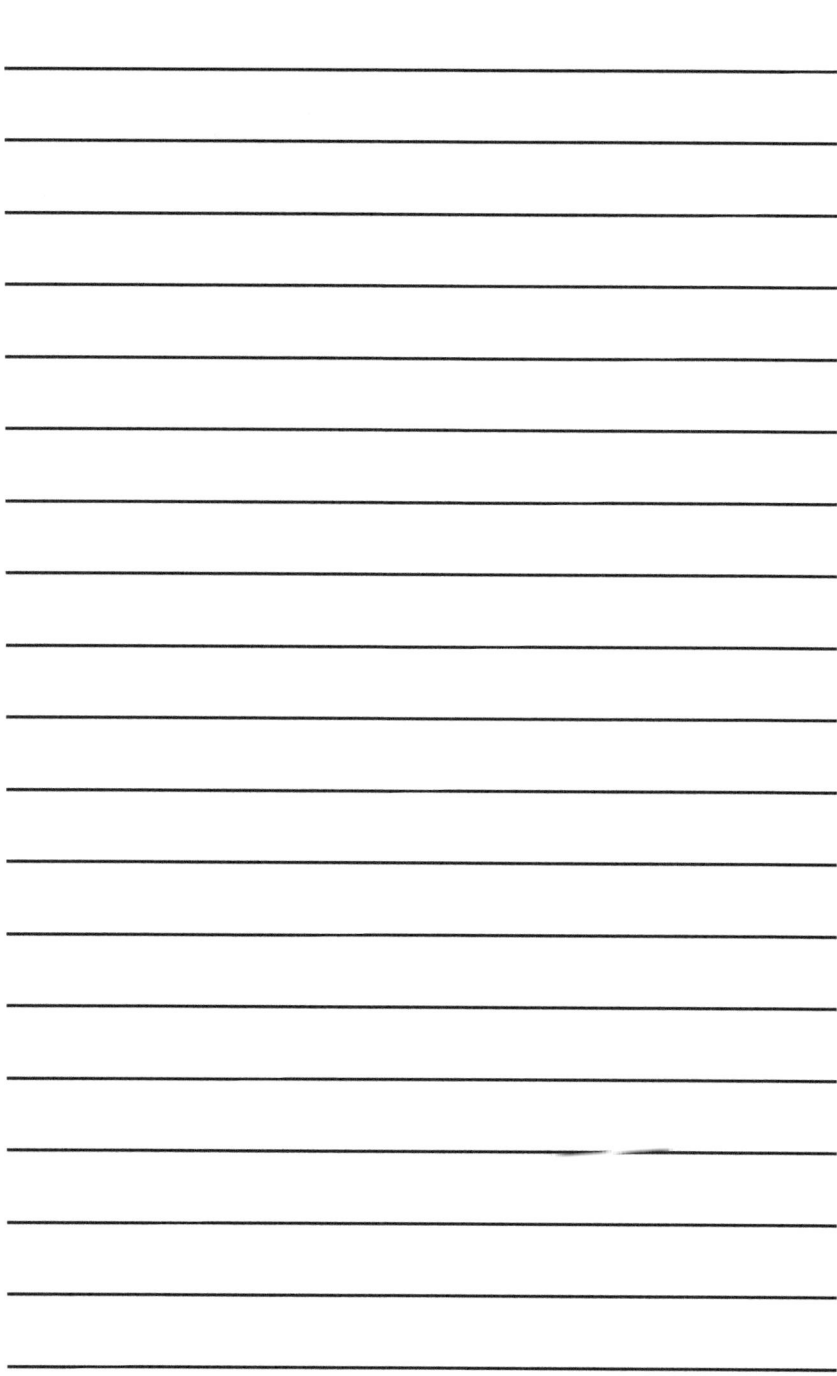

You have written for seven days!

Celebrate!

DON'T STOP NOW!
Keep going!

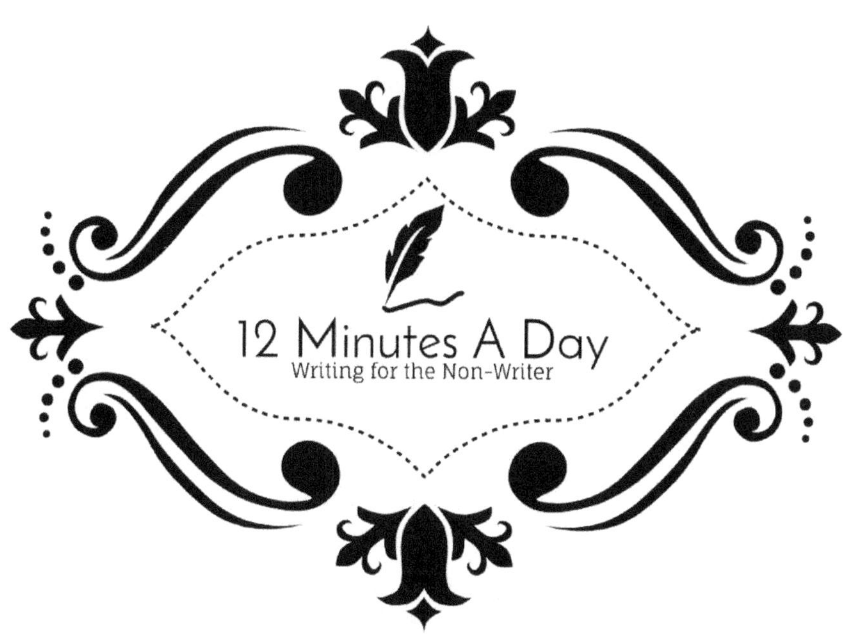

NUMBER 8

It's Easter. How do you and your family celebrate? What is important to you about this holiday?

DRAW IT BELOW

WRITE THE BLOG

NUMBER 9 

Have you ever visited a museum? Write about something you discovered and how it affected you.

DRAW IT BELOW

WRITE THE BLOG

NUMBER 10 

Think of something you could give away. Write about it and why you decided on that particular giveaway.

DRAW IT BELOW

WRITE THE BLOG

NUMBER 11 

Who is your favorite movie star? Why? What movies would you recommend your clients see that star this person?

DRAW IT BELOW

WRITE THE BLOG

NUMBER 12

Write a thank you to your favorite customer. Explain in detail why they are being showcased and what you love about them.

DRAW IT BELOW

WRITE THE BLOG

NUMBER 13

Do you have a new product? Highlight the details and write about the reason you developed this product. What will it do to help your customers?

DRAW IT BELOW

WRITE THE BLOG

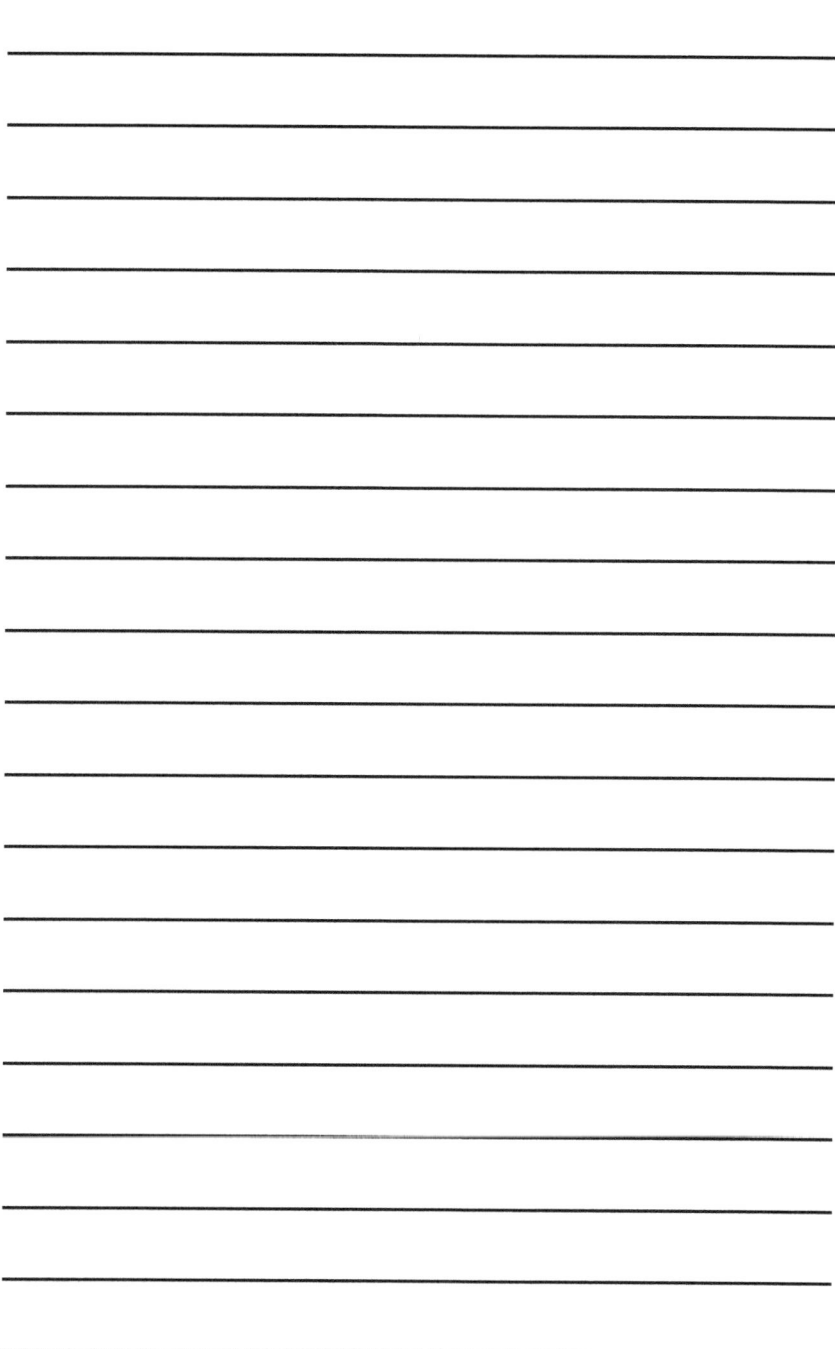

CONGRATULATIONS!
You have written for fourteen days!

NOW call yourself a blogger!

You are halfway there!

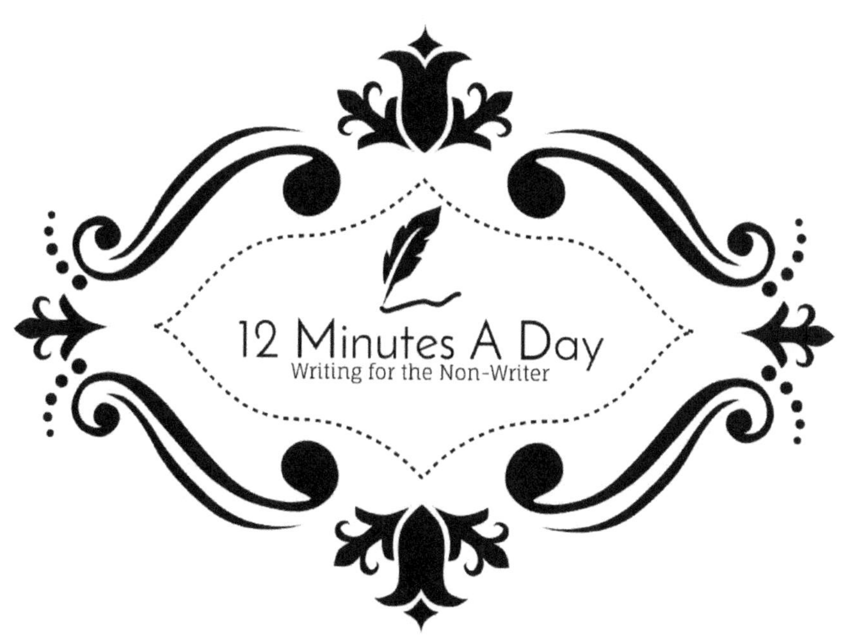
12 Minutes A Day
Writing for the Non-Writer

NUMBER 14 

Do you think that new technology is always a good thing? Write about an example where it has done more harm than good.

DRAW IT BELOW

WRITE THE BLOG

NUMBER 15 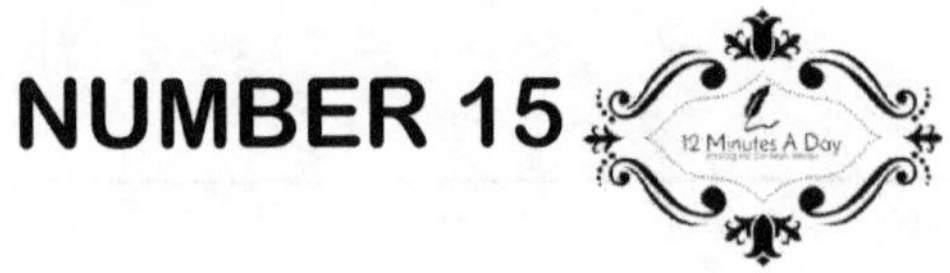

Make a list of things you wish you'd known when you first started your business. Then explain why these would be helpful for someone else starting out.

DRAW IT BELOW

WRITE THE BLOG

NUMBER 16 

What is your favorite business book? Explain how it's helped you and why your customers should read it.

DRAW IT BELOW

WRITE THE BLOG

NUMBER 17 

Write down questions you want to ask your customers about their experience. Tell them why you want the answers and how it will help your business.

DRAW IT BELOW

WRITE THE BLOG

NUMBER 18 

It's Veterans Day. Write a post about what that means to you. Be specific and if you know a veteran, write about them.

DRAW IT BELOW

WRITE THE BLOG

NUMBER 19 

Today is customer appreciation day! Write a thank letter to all your customers. Detail exactly why they are so important to you and how they've helped you grow personally and professionally.

DRAW IT BELOW

WRITE THE BLOG

NUMBER 20

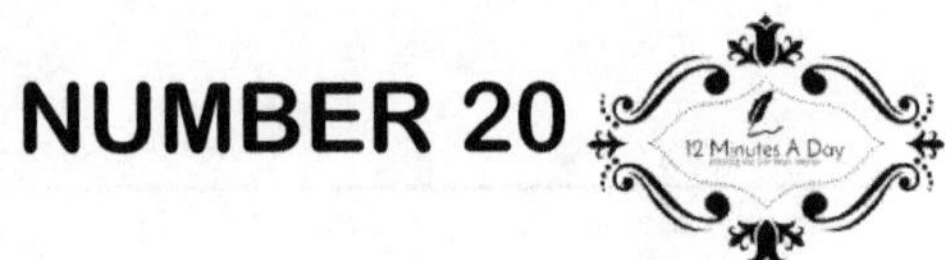

What do you think is the best invention of all time? Explain why you think so!

DRAW IT BELOW

WRITE THE BLOG

NUMBER 21 

What is the strangest thing you have ever seen? What were you doing when you saw it? Tell the story as if you are telling your best friend about it!

DRAW IT BELOW

WRITE THE BLOG

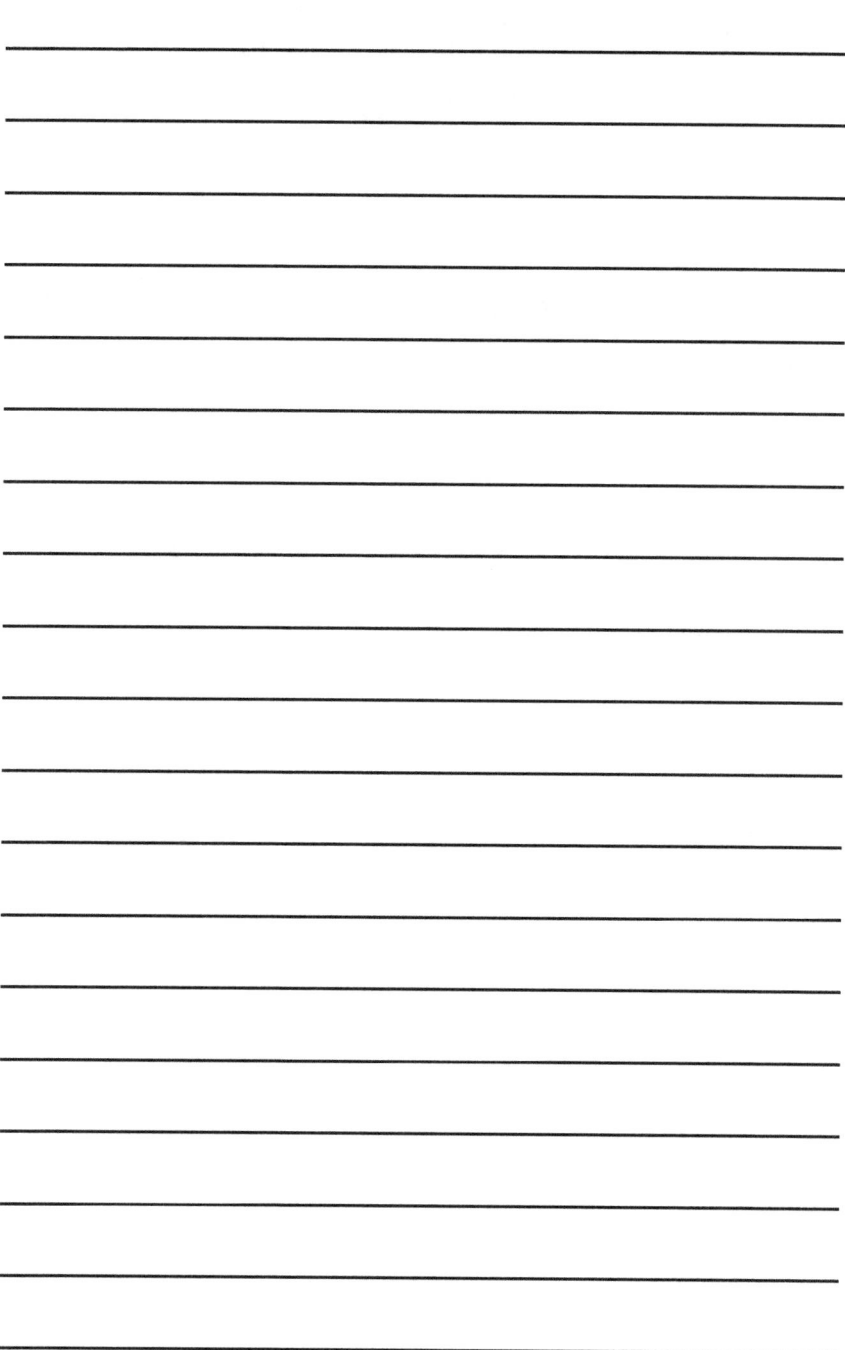

YOU ARE A ROCK STAR!

You've written twenty-one blogs!

Treat yourself to something nice!

You're almost there!
Keep writing!

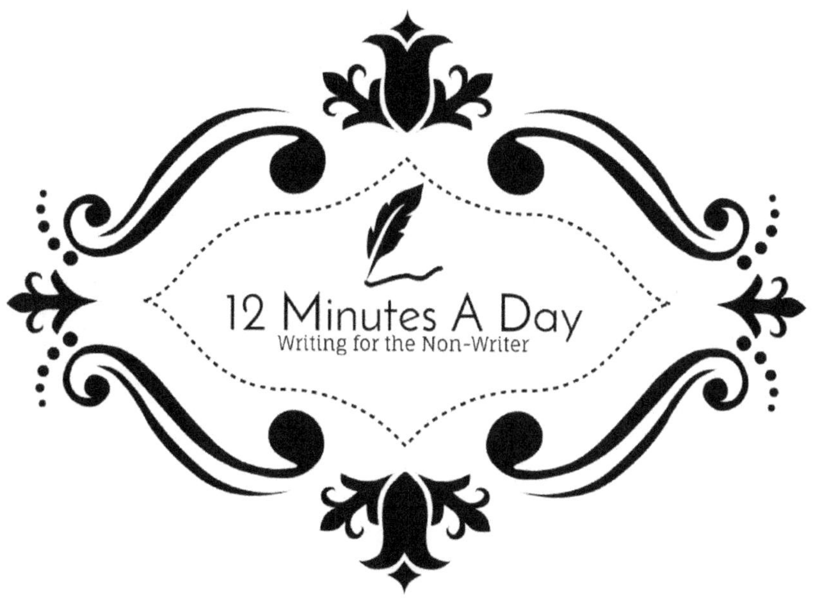

NUMBER 22 

What is your favorite vacation spot? Write a story about the spot and why it's your favorite. What would a typical day be like there?

DRAW IT BELOW

WRITE THE BLOG

NUMBER 23 

Do you have a peer that inspires you? Write about that person and why they are so inspirational.

DRAW IT BELOW

WRITE THE BLOG

NUMBER 24

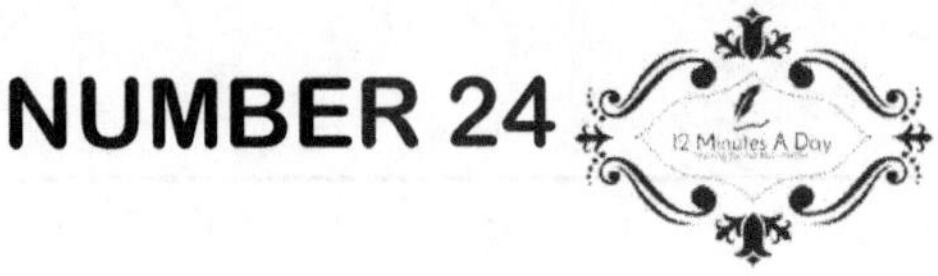

"When life gives you lemons, make lemonade." Describe what that phrase means to you. Do you have a life example of this? What happened?

DRAW IT BELOW

WRITE THE BLOG

NUMBER 25

Is there something most people don't know about you? Write about it in detail.

DRAW IT BELOW

WRITE THE BLOG

NUMBER 26

When you were growing up, did you have a favorite television show? What was most memorable about it? Why would you recommend someone watch it today?

DRAW IT BELOW

WRITE THE BLOG

NUMBER 27

Did you ever have a memorable customer service experience? Write about it. What do you think made it the most memorable? How did you apply that knowledge to your business?

DRAW IT BELOW

WRITE THE BLOG

NUMBER 28

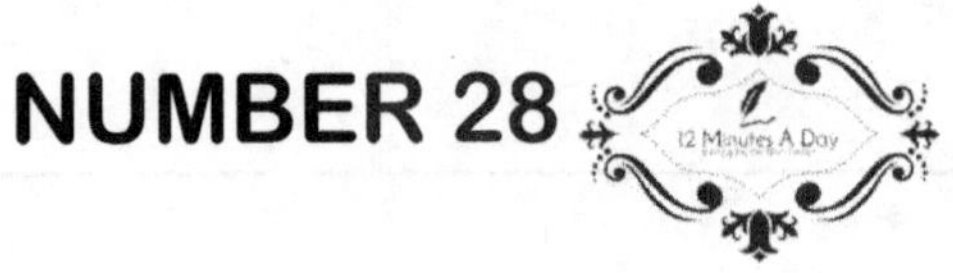

Write a story about the day you forgot something very important. What did you forget? What happened? How did you decide to remember next time?

DRAW IT BELOW

WRITE THE BLOG

NUMBER 29 

Do you have an easy life hack? Write about it. Use step by step instructions.

DRAW IT BELOW

WRITE THE BLOG

NUMBER 30 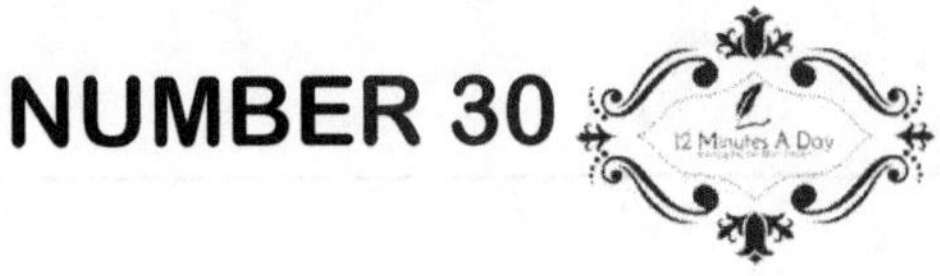

How has your industry grown since you started? Write about the pros and the cons and give your personal opinion on each of them.

DRAW IT BELOW

WRITE THE BLOG

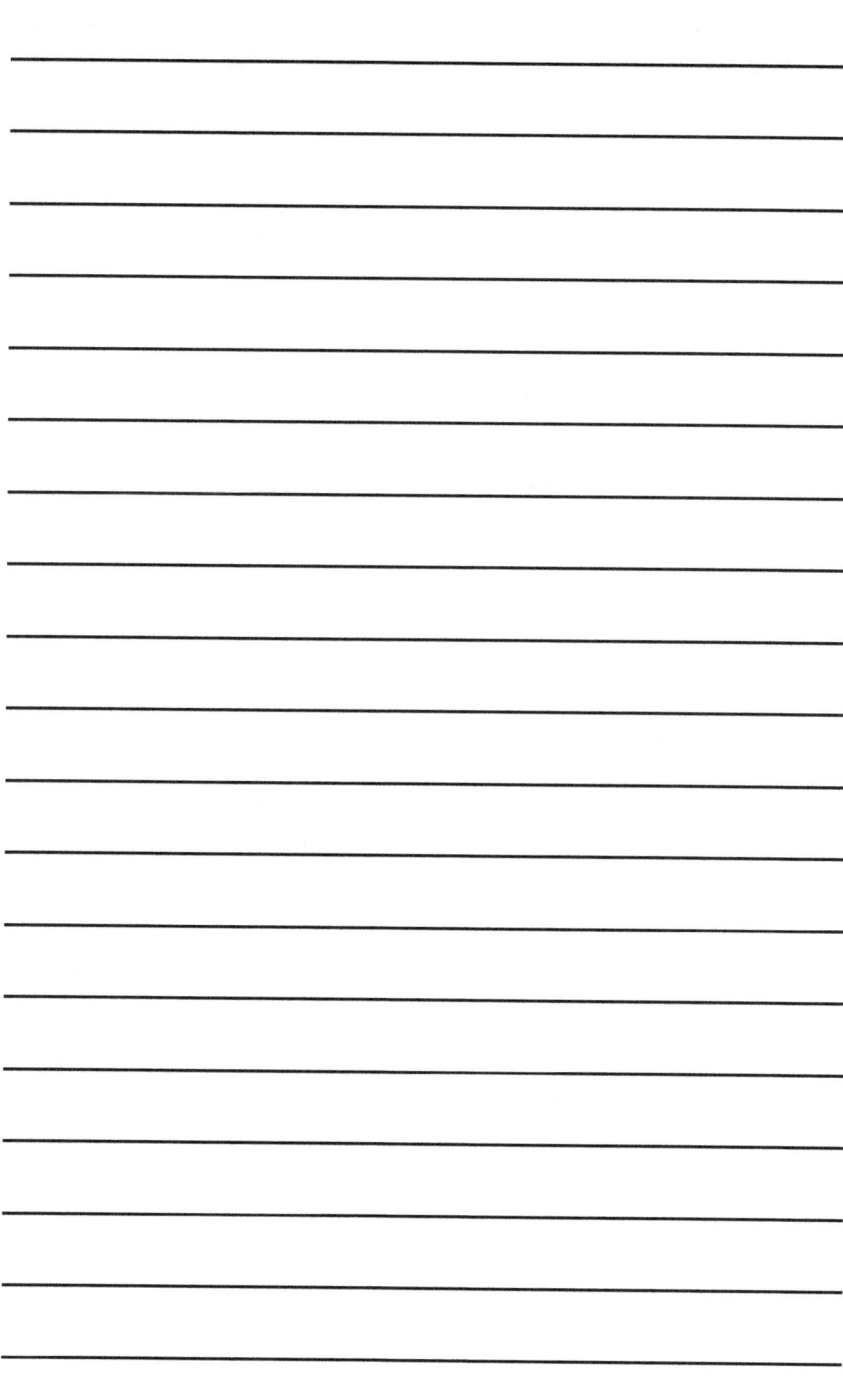

YOU ARE A BLOGGER! YOU have finished the 30 Day Writing Workout for Entrepreneurs! Now you have 30 days of blog posts!

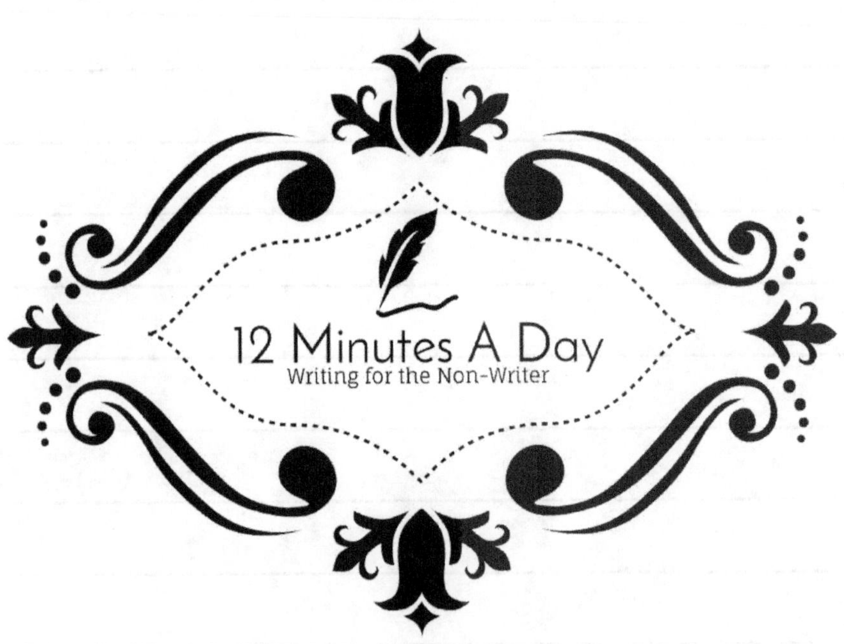

ABOUT THE AUTHOR

Renee Settle – Renee is a master coach, published author, and writer/editor consultant for hire. She is the inventor of 12 Minutes A Day, Writing for the Non-Writer. She is passionate about peoples stories and believes everyone has a story to write. She developed 12 Minutes A Day to help people do just that. Write their stories. Her motto is "Your Story Matters. My Story Matters. Together, our stories will change the world!" You can find her hanging out on her website at www.12minutestory.com.
Or at www.reneesettle.com

She can be found on social media:
Email: renee@reneesettle.com
Facebook (facebook.com/12minutestory)
Twitter (@12minutestory
Instagram (@12minutestory).

www.ingramcontent.com/pod-product-compliance
Lightning Source LLC
Chambersburg PA
CBHW061437180526
45170CB00004B/1443

* 9 7 8 1 5 4 0 7 0 1 2 8 2 *